Heaven Moves When You Pray

Unlocking the Power of a Conversation with God

By
Pastor Henry Owens Jr

Table of content

Foreword

There are moments in life when words fall short, when the weight of our burdens seems too heavy to bear, and the silence of heaven feels deafening. It is in those moments—when faith trembles and hope flickers—that prayer becomes not just a spiritual discipline, but a lifeline.

In Heaven Moves When You Pray, Pastor Henry Owens Jr. pulls back the veil on one of the greatest mysteries and privileges in the Christian life: the power of prayer that moves the heart of God. This is not a book of empty clichés or mechanical formulas. It is a divine revelation born from decades of walking with God through mountaintops and valleys alike—a testament to the reality that when a child of God prays, heaven listens and responds.

Pastor Owens writes with a voice shaped by forty years of ministry, soaked in Scripture and refined by experience. His teachings remind us that prayer is not an obligation; it is an invitation. It is the sacred meeting place between human weakness and divine strength. With passion and clarity, he shows that effective prayer doesn't begin with eloquence—it begins with intimacy. It begins when we realize that God's ear is tuned to the cries of His people.

Throughout these pages, you'll discover biblical truths and timeless principles that will reignite your prayer life. You will see how prayer unlocks doors that human effort cannot open, how it shifts atmospheres, restores families, breaks generational curses, and brings supernatural breakthrough where there once was impossibility. Pastor Owens reminds us that the prayers of the righteous do not evaporate—they accumulate, ascending before the throne like incense, until heaven itself moves in response.

As you read this book, prepare to be stirred, challenged, and transformed. Prepare to rediscover the joy of communing with your Creator. And remember this unshakable truth: prayer doesn't just change things—it changes you. And when you change, everything around you must change.

Heaven truly moves when you pray.

— From the Preface

Dedication

I want to dedicate this book to my Lord and Savior, Jesus Christ, who taught us that men ought always to pray and not lose heart.

To my beloved wife, Latrice L. Owens—thank you for your steadfast love, encouragement, and prayers. You are my rock and my partner in every season of life.

To my daughters, Tatiyanna L. Owens and Brittany M. Owens/Ellis, and to my seven beautiful granddaughters—Amiyah Jackson, Layanna Ellis, A'sani Ellis, Serenity Ellis, Grace Ellis, Zyiah Ellis, and Zariah Matthews—you are the joy of my heart. May your lives always reflect the power of prayer and the presence of God.

This book is also dedicated to every believer who has ever prayed through tears, trusted through pain, and worshiped through the storm. Heaven moves when you pray.

Acknowledgment

I want to acknowledge my Lord and Savior, Jesus Christ, for His wisdom, strength, and unfailing grace that made this book possible.

To my wife, Latrice L. Owens, my lifelong ministry partner—your love, patience, and faith have been a constant source of strength. To my daughters, Tatiyanna Owens and Brittany Ellis, and my granddaughters—Amiyah, Layanna, A'sani, Serenity, Grace, Zyiah, and Zariah—you are my daily inspiration and proof that God answers prayer.

My spiritual parents, Pastor Glenn and Gwen Taylor of Reno, Nevada—thank you for decades of encouragement and covering.

To Elder Waterford of Los Angeles, who helped me obtain my ministry license, and Minister Bowers, who encouraged me to preach as a young man, thank you for helping to ignite the fire that still burns in my heart today.

To my mother, Clester Willis-Jefferson, and her twin sister, Vester Moore, whose legacy of faith and evangelism continues to inspire me—your prayers laid the foundation for generations. To my late sister, Patricia Owens, and my sisters Myrdle Broughton and Samantha Butler, thank you for your love and support.

Finally, to my brothers and sisters in life and ministry—Lenard and Monique Dotson, Matthew and Rhonda Knight, Anthony and Loretta Velasquez, Vincent Stewart, Glenn Taylor II, Eddie Butler, Mitchell and Geishula Moore Jr., Terrell and Tara Taylor, and Tabu and Ebony McKnight—thank you for walking this journey of faith and prayer alongside me.

About the Author

Pastor Henry Owens Jr. was called to preach the gospel at the age of twelve and has served faithfully in ministry for over forty years. Throughout his life, he has sought to teach believers how to walk in spiritual authority, faith, and prayer.

A lifelong student of Scripture, Pastor Owens has spent more than thirty years studying the prophetic books of Daniel and Revelation, gaining deep insights into the end-time work of the Spirit and the power of intercession.

He currently ministers through Word and Spirit Ministries, where he teaches live Bible study sessions on YouTube and Facebook, reaching audiences across the globe. His teaching is rooted in the Word of God, rich in revelation, and anointed with compassion.

Pastor Owens has been married to his wife, Latrice L. Owens, for thirty-five years, and together they have raised two daughters and celebrate seven granddaughters. His passion is to see the church return to prayer, revival, and power—to see the people of God live victorious lives through faith in Jesus Christ.

Synopsis

Heaven Moves When You Pray is a divine call to believers everywhere to rediscover the true power of prayer. In this life-changing book, Pastor Henry Owens Jr. reveals that prayer is not a ritual but a relationship; not a duty, but a divine privilege.

Through Scripture, testimony, and revelation, this book shows how prayer connects heaven and earth—how the moment we bow our heads in faith, all of heaven leans in to listen. Pastor Owens explains how to develop a consistent prayer life, how to pray with authority, and how to overcome doubt and distraction in the secret place.

Readers will learn:

How to approach God with faith and confidence.

The difference between praying for something and praying through something.

Why persistence in prayer produces supernatural results.

How intercession unlocks generational blessings.

How worship and prayer work together to shift spiritual atmospheres.

If you've ever wondered whether your prayers matter, this book will assure you—they do. Heaven still moves when you pray.

Introduction:
Heaven Moves When You Pray

📖 *Jeremiah 33:3 – "Call unto Me, and I will answer you and show you great and mighty things you do not know."*

The Invitation to the Miraculous

What if I told you that **your words have the power to move heaven**? What if every whisper, every cry, every heartfelt plea you made in prayer was not only heard but had the ability to **shift circumstances, transform lives, and alter history**?

Prayer is **not a ritual**. It is not merely a religious practice we engage in before meals or before we sleep. Prayer is a divine **connection**—a supernatural conversation between you and the God who created the universe. When you pray, **you engage in heaven's agenda**. When you pray, **you open the doors for miracles**. When you pray, **God moves**.

Prayer is **not about fancy words**; it is about **real faith. Heaven does not respond to eloquence—heaven responds to faith.** The enemy of your soul fears nothing more than a believer who truly understands the **power of prayer**. Because when a person begins to pray in **faith, persistence, and expectation**, strongholds are broken, chains are shattered, and mountains are moved.

Prayer is the Key to Divine Intervention

📖 *James 5:16 – "The prayer of a righteous person is powerful and effective."*

God is not silent. He is listening. He is waiting. But the question is—are you praying?

Many believers struggle because they do **not yet understand the power they hold in prayer**. Some pray **doubtfully**—wondering if God even hears them. Others pray **halfheartedly**, never expecting much to change. And then there are those who **pray with authority, persistence, and unwavering faith**—and they see God move in ways that defy human understanding.

This book is an invitation to become that person.

- The one who prays with confidence
- The one who prays and sees results
- The one who prays not just to speak, but to move heaven

Throughout the Bible, we see that **nothing happens without prayer**. God's greatest interventions in history have come through the **prayers of His people**.

✓ Elijah prayed, and fire fell from heaven. (1 Kings 18:36-38)

✓ Hannah prayed, and her barren womb was opened. (1 Samuel 1:10-20)

✓ Daniel prayed, and an angel was sent to deliver him. (Daniel 6:22)

✓ The early church prayed, and Peter was released from prison. (Acts 12:5-10)

✓ Jesus prayed, and the blind saw, the dead were raised, and demons fled. (Luke 5:16, John 11:41-43)

And today, God is waiting for you to pray.

Heaven Responds to the Voice of the Faithful

📖 *Matthew 7:7 – "Ask, and it will be given to you; seek, and you will find; knock, and the door will be opened to you."*

There is a **spiritual war** raging over your life, your family, your future, and your destiny. Satan is not afraid of **Christians who go to church but never pray.** He is terrified of **believers who know how to wield the weapon of prayer.**

- Prayer opens closed doors.
- Prayer releases divine healing.
- Prayer dismantles demonic attacks.
- Prayer shifts the impossible into the possible.
- Prayer activates the will of God on earth.

If we truly understood the **authority we have in prayer**, we would never cease to pray. If we could **see in the spiritual realm** what happens when we pray, we would fall on our knees and never stop calling upon God.

But here's the hard truth: **Many people only pray when they are desperate.**

They only pray when they have exhausted all human solutions. They only seek God when **their strength has failed, their finances have dried up, or their relationships have fallen apart.**

But prayer was never meant to be our **last resort**—it was meant to be our **first response**.

What This Book Will Teach You

📖 *1 John 5:14-15 – "This is the confidence we have in approaching God: that if we ask anything according to His will, He hears us. And if we know that He hears us—whatever we ask—we know that we have what we asked of Him."*

This book is designed to **unlock the power of prayer in your life**. Each chapter will take you deeper into:

✓ Why prayer is essential to the Christian life
✓ The types of prayers that move heaven
✓ How faith and prayer work together
✓ The secrets to praying with authority and boldness
✓ How to persevere in prayer until you see results
✓ The joy and confidence that come from answered prayer

By the time you finish this book, you will no longer pray the same. Your prayers will be filled with power. Your words will carry divine authority. You will pray and expect heaven to move.

Because when you truly understand the **power of prayer**, you will never live a powerless life again.

Are You Ready to Pray Like Never Before?

📖 *Luke 18:1 – "Then Jesus told His disciples a parable to show them that they should always pray and not give up."*

If you have ever wondered:

• Does God really hear my prayers?
• Why do some people see miracles and others do not?
• How can I know I'm praying the right way?

Then this book is for you.

You were created to **speak and see mountains move**. You were made to **pray and expect answers**. You were born again not to live in spiritual defeat—but to walk in supernatural power.

🔥 **Are you ready to experience prayer that changes everything?**

🔥 **Are you ready to see heaven move when you pray?**

Then turn the page.

It's time to pray **with power**.

It's time to pray **with faith**.

It's time to **move heaven with your prayers**.

Because when you pray in faith, **God answers**.

📖 *James 5:16 – "The prayer of a righteous person is powerful and effective."*

🏰 **Let's begin.** 🏰

🔥 **What This Opening Accomplishes:**

✅ Captures attention **immediately**

✅ Establishes **urgency** and **authority** in prayer

✅ Inspires readers to **expect results** when they pray

✅ Sets a **powerful foundation** for the rest of the book

This introduction will grab the reader's heart and make them want to pray with expectation as they continue through the book.

Chapter 1:
The Purpose and Power of Prayer

📖 *1 Thessalonians 5:17 – "Pray without ceasing."*

Prayer is more than just words spoken into the air. It is a divine conversation between humanity and God—an invitation to engage with the Creator of the universe. Every time we pray, we enter into a spiritual exchange where heaven meets earth, where faith is strengthened, and where God's will is made manifest in our lives.

This chapter will explore:

✅ Why did God give us prayer?

✅ What happens in the spiritual realm when we pray?

✅ How does prayer build a relationship with God?

1. Why Did God Give Us Prayer?

📖 *Jeremiah 33:3 – "Call unto Me, and I will answer you and show you great and mighty things you do not know."*

God gave us prayer as a direct **connection to Him**. It is not merely a tool for **requests** but a means of **relationship, intimacy, and spiritual alignment**. Through prayer, we grow in our knowledge of God, receive His guidance, and experience His power in our daily lives.

A Divine Invitation

◆ Prayer is not just about speaking—it is about communion with God.

◆ Prayer brings our hearts into alignment with God's heart.

◆ God invites us into prayer so that we can experience His presence and hear His voice.

📖 *Isaiah 65:24 – "Before they call, I will answer; while they are still speaking, I will hear."*

Why God Created Prayer:

- To build a personal relationship with Him (James 4:8)
- To give us direct access to His wisdom (Proverbs 3:5-6)
- To align our will with His will (Matthew 6:10)
- To release His power into our circumstances (James 5:16)
- To strengthen our spirit and faith (Jude 1:20)

📖 **Biblical Example: Adam and Eve's Communication with God** (*Genesis 3:8-9*)

✅ Before the fall, Adam and Eve had **direct communion** with God in the Garden of Eden. Prayer restores that divine connection.

📖 **What This Means for You:** Prayer is not a religious duty—it is a **privilege** that gives you access to the very throne of God.

2. What Happens in the Spiritual Realm When We Pray?

📖 *Ephesians 6:12 – "For we do not wrestle against flesh and blood, but against rulers, against authorities, against the powers of this dark world and against the spiritual forces of evil in the heavenly realms."*

Every time you pray, something shifts in the unseen world. Prayer is not just words—it is spiritual warfare, divine activation, and supernatural transformation.

Prayer Activates Heaven's Power

◆ Prayer releases angelic intervention. (Daniel 10:12-14)

◆ Prayer dismantles the enemy's plans. (Luke 10:19)

◆ Prayer shifts spiritual atmospheres. (Acts 16:25-26)

📖 Biblical Example: Daniel's 21-Day Prayer Battle (*Daniel 10:12-14*)

✓ Daniel's prayers caused a heavenly battle—his answer was delayed because of spiritual warfare, but his persistence led to breakthrough.

Understanding the Spiritual Impact of Prayer

• Prayers invite God's presence into situations.
• Prayers release angelic assignments.
• Prayers break demonic strongholds.
• Prayers align our spirit with divine wisdom.

📖 What Happens in the Spirit When We Pray?

✓ When you pray in faith, you activate divine intervention.

✓ Heaven moves on your behalf when your prayers align with God's will.

🕮 **Testimony:** A woman who prayed for her prodigal son every day for **10 years**, and he finally came back to Christ.

3. How Does Prayer Build a Relationship with God?

🕮 *James 4:8 – "Draw near to God, and He will draw near to you."*

Prayer is the **language of relationship**. The more we pray, the **closer we get to God**. Imagine a friendship where you never talk to the other person—how strong would that relationship be? The same applies to our relationship with God.

Jesus Modeled a Life of Prayer

🕮 **Biblical Example: Jesus Praying in the Wilderness (*Luke 5:16*)**

✓ Even though Jesus was **fully God**, He still prayed **regularly** to the Father for strength, guidance, and communion.

🕮 *John 17:3 – "Now this is eternal life: that they know You, the only true God, and Jesus Christ, whom You have sent."*

The More You Pray, the More You Know God

◆ Prayer is more than talking—it is listening.

◆ Prayer reveals God's heart and mind.

◆ Prayer strengthens spiritual intimacy.

🕮 Real-Life Testimony: A pastor who spent years praying every morning at 4 AM, and as a result, he experienced supernatural encounters with God's presence.

4. The Power of Daily Prayer

📖 Matthew 6:6 – "When you pray, go into your room, close the door and pray to your Father, who is unseen. Then your Father, who sees what is done in secret, will reward you."

Prayer is not a **once-in-a-while event**—it is meant to be a **daily practice** that strengthens our spirit.

Why Should We Pray Daily?

📖 *Psalm 5:3 – "In the morning, Lord, You hear my voice; in the morning I lay my requests before You and wait expectantly."*

✔ **Daily prayer builds consistency.**

✔ **Daily prayer sharpens spiritual sensitivity.**

✔ **Daily prayer keeps us connected to God's voice.**

📖 Biblical Example: The Daily Prayers of the Early Church (*Acts 2:42*)

✔ The early church was devoted to prayer, and as a result, they witnessed signs, wonders, and supernatural growth.

📖 **What This Means for You:** If you desire a stronger relationship with God, begin setting **a daily prayer habit**.

5. The Lifeline of Every Believer

📖 *Colossians 4:2 – "Devote yourselves to prayer, being watchful and thankful."*

Prayer is **the lifeline of every believer**. It is the source of strength, wisdom, and power for those who want to live a victorious Christian life.

What Happens When We Stop Praying?

- ◆ We become spiritually weak.

- ◆ We lose divine direction.

- ◆ We give the enemy access.

📖 **Biblical Example: Samson's Neglected Prayer Life** (*Judges 16:20*)

✔ Samson lost his power because he stopped depending on God. **His downfall began when he neglected prayer and obedience.**

What Happens When We Pray?

✔ **We grow in faith.**

✔ **We receive divine insight.**

✔ **We experience supernatural breakthroughs.**

📖 **Testimony:** A man who was diagnosed with a **terminal illness** but received miraculous healing after a **church fasted and prayed for him for 30 days**.

Conclusion: The Power of Your Prayer Life

📖 *James 5:16 – "The prayer of a righteous person is powerful and effective."*

🔥 When you pray, heaven moves.

🔥 When you pray, miracles happen.

🔥 When you pray, the enemy flees.

Prayer is not **optional**—it is the **lifeline of the believer**. It is through **prayer** that we access God's power, **hear His voice**, and **see His hand at work** in our lives.

📖 **Challenge:** Will you commit to a **consistent** and **powerful** prayer life?

🕌 **Begin today. Heaven is waiting.** 🕌

Chapter 2:
The Foundation of Effective Prayer

📖 Matthew 6:9-13 – The Lord's Prayer

Prayer is the **lifeline** of a believer, but not all prayers are equally effective. Jesus, in His wisdom, provided a **model of powerful prayer** known as **The Lord's Prayer**, which serves as the perfect blueprint for how we should approach God.

This chapter will explore:

✅ Why did Jesus teach this model?

✅ How does it reveal the structure of powerful prayer?

✅ What happens in the spirit when we pray?

When we follow the biblical foundation of effective prayer, we don't just **speak words**—we activate heaven's power, align ourselves with God's will, and experience **supernatural results**.

1. Why Did Jesus Teach This Model?

📖 Luke 11:1 – "One day Jesus was praying in a certain place. When He finished, one of His disciples said to Him, 'Lord, teach us to pray.'"

Jesus' disciples saw His powerful life of prayer and recognized that His authority, wisdom, and miracles were directly connected to

His prayer life. Unlike the Pharisees, who prayed to be seen, Jesus prayed to connect with the Father.

Key Reasons Jesus Gave Us This Model:

✦ To teach us how to approach God with reverence. (*Psalm 100:4*)

✦ To show us that prayer is about alignment, not just requests. (*Matthew 6:33*)

✦ To demonstrate that prayer is a relationship, not a ritual. (*John 15:7*)

📖 **Biblical Example: Moses Speaking with God** (*Exodus 33:11*)

✅ "The Lord would speak to Moses face to face, as one speaks to a friend."

Jesus did not give us empty words but a structure of communication that teaches us how to engage in powerful and effective prayer.

📖 What This Means for You: Prayer is more than words—it is the foundation of an intimate relationship with God.

2. The Structure of Powerful Prayer (Breaking Down the Lord's Prayer)

📖 Matthew 6:9-13

Each line of **The Lord's Prayer** is filled with **spiritual depth** and **heavenly power**. Let's break it down:

◆ **Recognizing God's Holiness – "Our Father, Who Art in Heaven, Hallowed Be Thy Name"**

📖 *Psalm 96:9* – "Worship the Lord in the splendor of His holiness."

Before anything else, **prayer begins with worship**. When we approach God, we must:

✓ Acknowledge His greatness.

✓ Enter His presence with reverence.

✓ Recognize His holiness and majesty.

📖 Biblical Example: Isaiah's Vision of God's Glory (Isaiah 6:1-5)

✓ **Isaiah saw God's holiness and responded in awe and reverence.**

📖 *What Happens in the Spirit? – When we begin with praise and worship, we shift our focus from our problems to God's power.*

◆ **Surrendering to His Will – "Thy Kingdom Come, Thy Will Be Done"**

📖 *Matthew 26:39* – "Not My will, but Yours be done."

Effective prayer is **not about forcing our will on God**—it is about aligning ourselves **with His will**. This is why Jesus prayed:

✓ For God's Kingdom to be established on earth.

✓ For His will to be done, not our own.

10

✅ For us to walk in obedience to His plans.

📖 *Biblical Example: Jesus Praying in Gethsemane (Matthew 26:36-46)*

✅ *Jesus surrendered His own will to fulfill the Father's perfect plan.*

📖 What Happens in the Spirit? – When we submit to God's will, we unlock divine favor and heavenly intervention.

◆ **Trusting in His Provision – "Give Us This Day Our Daily Bread"**

📖 *Philippians 4:19* – "And my God will supply all your needs according to His riches in glory in Christ Jesus."

God is **our Provider**. When we pray, we should trust that He will:

✅ Meet our daily needs.

✅ Supply wisdom, strength, and direction.

✅ Provide for us physically, emotionally, and spiritually.

📖 Biblical Example: Manna in the Wilderness (*Exodus 16:4-35*)

✅ The Israelites received fresh manna daily—a sign that God provides exactly what we need, when we need it.

📖 What Happens in the Spirit? – When we pray for provision with faith, heaven releases what we need for today.

◆ The Power of Forgiveness – "And Forgive Us Our Debts, as We Forgive Our Debtors"

📖 *Mark 11:25* – "When you stand praying, if you hold anything against anyone, forgive them."

Unforgiveness **blocks prayers**. Jesus taught that:

✓ We must forgive to be forgiven.

✓ Bitterness hinders spiritual growth.

✓ Forgiveness releases healing and breakthrough.

📖 Biblical Example: Joseph Forgiving His Brothers (Genesis 50:19-21)

✓ Joseph's forgiveness led to family restoration and divine favor.

📖 What Happens in the Spirit? – When we forgive, chains of offense are broken, and God's peace fills our hearts.

◆ Seeking Protection – "And Lead Us Not into Temptation, But Deliver Us from Evil"

📖 2 Thessalonians 3:3 – "The Lord is faithful, and He will strengthen you and protect you from the evil one."

God wants to protect us from spiritual attacks. This part of prayer reminds us to:

✓ Ask for divine protection.

✓ Remain watchful against the enemy's schemes.

✅ Walk in God's supernatural covering.

📖 Biblical Example: Job's Hedge of Protection (Job 1:10)

✅ God placed a divine hedge around Job—until Satan sought permission to attack.

📖 What Happens in the Spirit? – When we pray for God's protection, we invite divine shielding from harm.

3. Biblical Example: Hannah's Prayer for a Son

📖 1 Samuel 1:10-20

Hannah desperately wanted a child, but she was barren. Instead of complaining, she prayed in faith and made a vow to the Lord.

✅ She poured her heart out to God. (1 Samuel 1:10)

✅ She made a commitment to dedicate her child to God. (1 Samuel 1:11)

✅ She left with peace, trusting in God's answer. (1 Samuel 1:18)

📖 What This Means for You: When we pray with faith, God answers in His perfect timing.

4. What Happens in the Spirit When We Pray?

📖 *Revelation 8:3-4* – "The smoke of the incense, together with the prayers of God's people, went up before God from the angel's hand."

Every time you pray, your words rise before God like incense.

Spiritual Realities of Prayer:

✅ Heaven hears and records every prayer. (Revelation 5:8)

✅ Angels respond to prayers of faith. (Daniel 10:12-14)

✅ Demonic strongholds are broken through persistent prayer. (2 Corinthians 10:4)

📖 Testimony: A pastor prayed for a revival in his city for 25 years. One day, a supernatural outpouring of the Holy Spirit swept through his church, and thousands came to Christ.

📖 What Happens in the Spirit? – When we pray, God moves behind the scenes, aligning circumstances for His glory.

Conclusion: The Power of a Well-Structured Prayer Life

📖 *James 5:16* – "The prayer of a righteous person is powerful and effective."

When you pray according to the biblical foundation Jesus gave, your prayers become powerful, effective, and unstoppable.

🔥 **Are you ready to pray with power?**

🔥 **Are you ready to see heaven move when you pray?**

Then begin today—because **prayer changes everything**.

🏰 **Start praying with boldness, and watch heaven respond.** 🏰

Chapter 3:
The Different Types of Prayer

📖 Philippians 4:6 – "By prayer and supplication with thanksgiving let your requests be made known to God."

Prayer is not one-dimensional—it is a vast and powerful tool that can be used in different ways depending on the need and circumstance. The Bible outlines various types of prayer, each with a unique purpose in our spiritual walk and relationship with God.

This chapter will explore:

✓ The different types of prayer and their biblical significance

✓ How and when to apply each type of prayer in your life

✓ What happens in the spirit when we use the right kind of prayer

Many believers struggle in their prayer life because they don't realize that prayer is multifaceted. Just as a soldier uses different weapons in battle, a believer must learn to use the right form of prayer for different situations.

1. Prayers of Thanksgiving

📖 *1 Thessalonians 5:18 – "Give thanks in all circumstances; for this is God's will for you in Christ Jesus."*

A prayer of thanksgiving focuses on praising God for who He is and what He has done. It shifts our focus from problems to gratitude and cultivates joy and faith.

Why Thanksgiving is Powerful:

◆ It magnifies **God's goodness** rather than our struggles.

◆ It strengthens **faith**—when we thank God for what He has done, we trust Him for what He will do.

◆ It invites **God's presence** into our lives.

📖 Biblical Example: Jesus Giving Thanks Before Multiplying the Loaves and Fish (John 6:11)

✓ Before performing a miracle, Jesus gave thanks, demonstrating that gratitude releases supernatural provision.

📖 Application: Make thanksgiving a daily habit in your prayers—thank God before you see the answer, and you will experience greater peace and joy.

2. Prayers of Intercession

📖 1 Timothy 2:1-2 – "I urge that petitions, prayers, intercessions, and thanksgiving be offered for all people—for kings and all those in authority."

Intercessory prayer is when **we pray on behalf of others**. It is an act of **spiritual advocacy**, standing in the gap for individuals, nations, or situations.

Why Intercession is Powerful:

◆ It invites **God's intervention** into people's lives.

◆ It protects and **covers others spiritually**.

◆ It reflects **Christ's heart**, as He constantly intercedes for us.

📖 Biblical Example: Moses' Intercession for Israel (*Exodus 32:11-14*)

✔ After Israel sinned by worshipping the golden calf, Moses stood in the gap and pleaded for God's mercy, and God relented.

📖 Application:

- Pray for your family, church, community, and leaders.
- Stand in prayer for those who cannot pray for themselves.
- Be persistent—intercession changes lives and shifts nations.

📖 **Real-Life Testimony:** A woman interceded for her husband's **salvation** for 20 years. One day, he surrendered his life to Christ, showing that **persistent intercession works**.

3. Prayers of Warfare

📖 Ephesians 6:12-18 – "For we wrestle not against flesh and blood, but against principalities, against powers, against the rulers of darkness of this world."

Spiritual warfare prayers are used to fight against demonic forces, oppression, and strongholds. These prayers are bold, authoritative, and based on Scripture.

Why Warfare Prayers are Powerful:

◆ They break demonic strongholds.

◆ They release divine protection.

◆ They bring spiritual victory over darkness.

📖 Biblical Example: Paul Casting Out a Spirit of Divination (Acts 16:16-18)

✓ Paul commanded a demonic spirit to leave a young girl, and immediately, she was set free.

📖 Application:

- Use **Scripture** in warfare prayers (*Luke 10:19*).
- Stand on **God's authority** to rebuke the enemy (*James 4:7*).
- Engage in **fasting and prayer** to break strongholds (*Isaiah 58:6*).

📖 Real-Life Testimony: A man who struggled with addiction prayed aggressively using spiritual warfare prayers and experienced supernatural deliverance.

4. Prayers of Agreement

📖 Matthew 18:19 – "If two of you agree on earth about anything they ask, it will be done for them by My Father in heaven."

Prayers of agreement involve two or more believers uniting in faith for a common request. There is power in corporate prayer, as it builds faith, unity, and spiritual authority.

Why Agreement Prayer is Powerful:

- ◆ It multiplies faith—there is strength in unity.

- ◆ It reinforces spiritual authority.

- ◆ It releases supernatural answers quickly.

📖 Biblical Example: The Early Church Praying for Peter's Release (Acts 12:5-12)

✅ The church gathered to pray, and God sent an angel to deliver Peter from prison.

📖 **Application:**

- Pray with your spouse, family, or church.
- Find a prayer partner to stand with you in agreement.
- Engage in corporate prayer meetings.

📖 Real-Life Testimony: A family facing financial struggles joined together in prayer of agreement, and soon after, a breakthrough came through an unexpected job opportunity.

5. Other Types of Prayer in the Bible

◆ Prayers of Repentance

📖 2 Chronicles 7:14 – "If My people, who are called by My name, will humble themselves and pray and seek My face and turn from their wicked ways, then I will hear from heaven."

✅ Example: The Prodigal Son repenting and returning home (Luke 15:18-20).

📖 **Application: When we sin, we should immediately turn to God in repentance.**

◆ Prayers of Dedication

📖 1 Samuel 1:27-28 – "For this child I prayed, and the Lord has granted me my petition."

19

✓ Example: Hannah dedicating Samuel to God (1 Samuel 1:27-28).

📖 **Application:** Dedicate your children, home, career, and future to God.

◆ **Prayers of Petition (Supplication)**

📖 Philippians 4:6 – "Do not be anxious about anything, but in every situation, by prayer and supplication, with thanksgiving, present your requests to God."

✓ Example: Hezekiah praying for healing (2 Kings 20:1-6).

📖 Application: Bring your needs before God, trusting in His provision.

6. Learning Which Prayer to Use in Different Situations

📖 *Ecclesiastes 3:1 – "To everything there is a season, a time for every purpose under heaven."*

◈ When you need spiritual breakthrough → Use prayers of warfare.

◈ When you are praying for others → Use intercessory prayer.

◈ When you need financial provision → Pray in agreement with others.

◈ When you want to strengthen your faith → Use prayers of thanksgiving.

📖 Biblical Example: Elijah Using Different Prayers at Different Times

✅ He prayed against evil (warfare) → 1 Kings 18:36-39

✅ He prayed for rain to return (petition) → 1 Kings 18:42-45

📖 What This Means for You: When you learn to pray strategically, you will see more answered prayers and greater spiritual breakthroughs.

7. Conclusion: The Power of Diversifying Your Prayer Life

📖 James 5:16 – "The prayer of a righteous person is powerful and effective."

🔥 **Prayer is not "one-size-fits-all."**

🔥 **Each type of prayer unlocks different realms of spiritual power.**

🔥 **When you pray effectively, heaven responds!**

🏰 **Start implementing different types of prayer today and watch how your spiritual life transforms.** 🏰

Chapter 4:
The Faith Connection in Prayer

📖 *Mark 11:24 – "Whatever you ask for in prayer, believe that you have received it, and it will be yours."*

Faith is the currency of heaven. Without faith, prayer lacks power, and without prayer, faith remains stagnant. Every answered prayer in the Bible was connected to faith-filled expectation. Jesus Himself emphasized that faith is the foundation for receiving from God.

This chapter will explore:

✅ Why faith is necessary for answered prayer

✅ How to grow in faith for stronger prayers

✅ Biblical and real-life examples of faith unlocking supernatural breakthroughs

Many Christians struggle with unanswered prayers because they pray without expectation. If faith is missing, prayer becomes empty words, but when faith is present, mountains move, miracles happen, and heaven responds.

1. Why is Faith Necessary for Answered Prayer?

📖 Hebrews 11:6 – "And without faith, it is impossible to please God, because anyone who comes to Him must believe that He exists and that He rewards those who earnestly seek Him."

Faith is not just believing that God exists—it is trusting that He is faithful to His promises. When we pray:

✅ We must believe God hears us. (1 John 5:14-15)

✅ We must trust that His Word is true. (Numbers 23:19)

✅ We must expect that His power is at work. (Ephesians 3:20)

📖 Biblical Example: Blind Bartimaeus' Faith (Mark 10:46-52)

✅ When Bartimaeus heard that Jesus was near, he shouted in faith, believing that Jesus could heal him. Jesus responded, "Your faith has healed you."

Faith Activates the Power of God

◆ Faith is the **key** that unlocks **miracles**.

◆ Faith brings **God's promises into reality**.

◆ Faith **removes doubt**, making room for divine answers.

📖 **Biblical Example: The Centurion's Faith (Matthew 8:5-13)**

✅ The Roman centurion didn't need Jesus to touch his servant—he believed that Jesus' Word alone was enough.

📖 What Happens in the Spirit? – When we pray with faith, angels move, heaven shifts, and the supernatural is released.

2. How Can We Grow in Faith?

Faith is like a **muscle**—it must be **exercised** and **developed** to grow stronger.

◆ Hearing and Meditating on the Word

📖 Romans 10:17 – "Faith comes by hearing, and hearing by the Word of God."

♦ Read Scripture daily to fill your mind with faith.

♦ Listen to testimonies and sermons to increase belief.

♦ Meditate on God's promises and declare them over your life.

📖 Biblical Example: Joshua Meditating on God's Word (Joshua 1:8)

✓ God told Joshua that meditating on the Word would guarantee success and victory.

◆ Praying with Expectation

📖 James 1:6 – "But when you ask, you must believe and not doubt."

♦ Pray as if the answer is already on its way.

♦ Speak faith-filled words, not fear and doubt.

♦ Trust that God's timing is perfect.

📖 Biblical Example: Elijah Praying for Rain (1 Kings 18:41-45)

✓ Elijah prayed persistently for rain, even when there was no visible sign of it. He kept praying until the answer came.

◆ Walking in Obedience

📖 2 Corinthians 5:7 – "For we walk by faith, not by sight."

Faith requires stepping out even when things don't make sense.

◆ Take action before you see results.

◆ Trust God's direction, even when it looks impossible.

📖 Biblical Example: Peter Walking on Water (Matthew 14:28-31)

✓ Peter walked by faith, but when he focused on circumstances, he began to sink.

📖 What Happens in the Spirit? – When we step out in faith, God meets us with supernatural provision and answers.

3. Biblical Example: The Woman with the Issue of Blood

📖 Mark 5:25-34

✓ A woman who suffered for 12 years pressed through a crowd to touch Jesus' garment.

✓ She believed that just touching Jesus' clothes would heal her.

✓ Jesus turned and said, "Daughter, your faith has made you well."

Faith Works Even Before You See the Answer

◆ The woman's faith was active before the healing took place.

◆ Jesus felt the power leave Him before He even saw her.

◆ Her faith demanded a response from heaven.

📖 Application: If you need healing, financial breakthrough, or restoration, pray boldly and expect heaven to move.

25

4. Real-Life Testimony: A Woman's Healing Through Faith

A woman was diagnosed with a terminal illness. Doctors gave her no hope. Instead of giving up, she:

✅ Prayed with faith every day, declaring healing.

✅ Refused to speak words of doubt.

✅ Worshipped and thanked God in advance for her healing.

Months later, she returned to the doctor, and to their shock, her test results showed no sign of the disease. Faith had activated God's healing power.

📖 Mark 9:23 – "Everything is possible for the one who believes."

📖 What Happens in the Spirit? – When faith is present, miracles manifest in the physical realm.

5. Why Some Prayers Go Unanswered

Sometimes, prayers are not answered immediately. Here's why:

◆ Doubt Cancels Faith

📖 Matthew 13:58 – "And He did not do many miracles there because of their lack of faith."

◆ Jesus could not perform miracles in His hometown because of unbelief.

📖 Biblical Example: Israelites in the Wilderness (Numbers 14:11)

✅ Their doubt kept them from entering the Promised Land.

◆ Praying Outside of God's Will

📖 1 John 5:14 – "If we ask anything according to His will, He hears us."

◆ If a prayer does not align with God's will, He may say "No" or "Not yet."

📖 Biblical Example: Paul's Thorn in the Flesh (2 Corinthians 12:7-9)

✅ Paul prayed for his suffering to be removed, but God told him, "My grace is sufficient for you."

◆ Lack of Persistence

📖 Luke 18:1 – "Jesus told His disciples a parable to show them that they should always pray and not give up."

◆ Some prayers require persistent faith.

◆ Keep praying until the breakthrough comes.

📖 Biblical Example: Daniel's Delayed Answer (Daniel 10:12-13)

✅ Daniel prayed for 21 days before his answer arrived, because spiritual warfare delayed it.

📖 What Happens in the Spirit? – Some prayers require persistent faith to break through spiritual opposition.

6. Conclusion: Faith-Powered Prayer Unlocks Miracles

📖 James 5:15 – "And the prayer offered in faith will make the sick person well."

🔥 **Faith is the missing link in many prayers.**

🔥 **When faith is activated, heaven moves.**

🔥 **Pray boldly, trust completely, and never doubt God's power.**

🏰 **Are you ready to pray with faith and see God move?** 🏰

Chapter 5:
The Conditions for Answered Prayer

📖 John 16:24 – "Ask, and you shall receive, that your joy may be full."

Many people pray, but not all prayers are answered. Have you ever wondered why some prayers bring breakthroughs while others seem to go unheard? The Bible teaches that prayer is not just about asking—it is about aligning with God's principles.

This chapter will explore:

✓ Why some prayers go unanswered

✓ What conditions must be met for God to respond

✓ How to pray effectively to see results

Prayer is not a magic formula—it is a spiritual partnership with God. When we pray correctly, heaven moves, angels respond, and God's power is released.

1. Why Do Some Prayers Go Unanswered?

📖 James 4:3 – "You ask and do not receive, because you ask amiss, that you may spend it on your pleasures."

Many people get frustrated when prayers are not answered, but the Bible provides clear reasons why this happens.

◆ Praying Outside of God's Will

📖 1 John 5:14 – "If we ask anything according to His will, He hears us."

♦ God will never grant a request that contradicts His will.

♦ Selfish prayers often go unanswered (James 4:3).

♦ The key to answered prayer is to align our desires with God's desires.

📖 Biblical Example: Jesus in Gethsemane (Matthew 26:39)

✅ Jesus prayed, "Not My will, but Yours be done."

📖 Application: Instead of demanding what we want, we should seek what God wants for us.

◆ Praying with Unconfessed Sin

📖 *Psalm 66:18* – "If I regard iniquity in my heart, the Lord will not hear me."

♦ Sin creates a barrier between us and God.

♦ Repentance restores communication with Him (Isaiah 59:1-2).

♦ A pure heart leads to powerful prayers.

📖 Biblical Example: The Pharisee and the Tax Collector (Luke 18:9-14)

✅ The Pharisee prayed pridefully, but the humble tax collector was heard because he repented.

📖 Application: Before asking for anything, ask God to cleanse your heart (1 John 1:9).

◆ **Lack of Faith**

📖 Mark 11:24 – "Whatever you ask for in prayer, believe that you have received it, and it will be yours."

◆ **Doubt blocks answers from heaven (James 1:6-7).**

◆ Faith activates the supernatural.

◆ If you don't expect an answer, you may never receive one.

📖 Biblical Example: Peter Walking on Water (Matthew 14:28-31)

✓ Peter started sinking when he let fear replace faith.

📖 Application: Approach God with confidence, not uncertainty (Hebrews 4:16).

◆ **Lack of Persistence**

📖 Luke 18:1 – "Men ought always to pray and not lose heart."

◆ Some prayers require ongoing intercession.

◆ Breakthroughs happen when we refuse to give up (Daniel 10:12-13).

◆ Delayed answers are often tests of perseverance.

📖 Biblical Example: Elijah Praying for Rain (1 Kings 18:41-45)

✓ Elijah prayed seven times before the rain came.

📖 Application: If you're praying for something and haven't received it yet, don't stop praying.

2. The Conditions for Answered Prayer

📖 *Matthew 21:22* – "If you believe, you will receive whatever you ask for in prayer."

If we want God to answer our prayers, we must follow **spiritual principles**.

◆ Condition #1: Pray According to God's Will

📖 Romans 12:2 – "Do not conform to the pattern of this world but be transformed by the renewing of your mind. Then you will be able to test and approve what God's will is—His good, pleasing, and perfect will."

✅ God's will is found in His Word.

✅ If we pray Scripture, we pray His will.

✅ God's will always brings glory to Him.

📖 Biblical Example: Solomon Asking for Wisdom (1 Kings 3:5-14)

✅ Solomon's request pleased God, so it was granted.

📖 Application: Instead of asking for your desires, ask God to reveal His will.

◆ Condition #2: Pray with a Pure Heart

📖 Matthew 5:8 – "Blessed are the pure in heart, for they shall see God."

✅ A clean heart leads to effective prayers.

✅ Forgiveness unlocks divine favor (Mark 11:25).

✅ Unforgiveness blocks blessings (Matthew 6:14-15).

📖 Biblical Example: Job Praying for His Friends (Job 42:10)

✅ Job was restored when he prayed for others.

📖 **Application: Before praying, ask God to purify your heart.**

◆ **Condition #3: Pray with Perseverance**

📖 Galatians 6:9 – "Let us not grow weary in doing good, for in due season we shall reap if we do not lose heart."

✅ Some answers require long-term faithfulness.

✅ Spiritual warfare can delay results (Daniel 10:12-13).

✅ God answers in His timing, not ours.

📖 Biblical Example: Hannah Praying for a Son (1 Samuel 1:10-20)

✅ Hannah prayed for years, and God gave her Samuel.

📖 Application: Don't quit—your answer may be closer than you think.

◆ **Condition #4: Pray with Thanksgiving**

📖 *Philippians 4:6* – "Do not be anxious about anything, but in every situation, by prayer and supplication, with thanksgiving, present your requests to God."

✅ Gratitude attracts more blessings.

✅ Thanking God before seeing results shows faith.

✅ Thanksgiving releases supernatural joy.

📖 Biblical Example: Jesus Giving Thanks Before Raising Lazarus   (John   11:41-44)
✅ Jesus thanked God first, and then Lazarus was resurrected.

📖 Application: Start thanking God before your answer comes.

◆ **Condition #5: Pray with Humility**

📖 James 4:10 – "Humble yourselves before the Lord, and He will lift you up."

✅ Arrogance blocks answers from heaven.

✅ Humility invites divine favor (1 Peter 5:6).

✅ God resists the proud (James 4:6).

📖 Biblical Example: The Canaanite Woman's Humility (Matthew 15:21-28)

✅ She humbly persisted, and Jesus granted her request.

📖 Application: Approach God with reverence and humility.

3. What Happens in the Spirit When We Pray?

📖 Revelation 8:3-4 – "The smoke of the incense, together with the prayers of God's people, went up before God from the angel's hand."

✅ Prayers are stored in heaven and released at the right time.

✅ Angels carry prayers before God.

✅ Spiritual warfare can delay answers (Daniel 10:12-13).

📖 Biblical Example: Cornelius' Prayers Bringing Divine Favor (Acts 10:1-4)

✅ Cornelius' consistent prayers and giving moved heaven.

📖 Application: Every prayer matters, even when the answer is delayed.

4. Conclusion: Aligning Yourself for Answered Prayer

📖 James 5:16 – "The prayer of a righteous person is powerful and effective."

🔥 **God wants to answer prayers, but He responds to those who follow His principles.**

🔥 **When you pray correctly, expect supernatural breakthroughs!**

🔥 **Are you ready to align your prayers with God's will?**

💼 **Start applying these conditions today and watch your prayer life transform!** 💼

Chapter 6:
The Battle of Spiritual
Warfare in Prayer

📖 Ephesians 6:12 – "For we wrestle not against flesh and blood, but against principalities, against powers, against the rulers of the darkness of this world, against spiritual wickedness in high places."

Prayer is not just communication with God—it is a weapon in the battle between good and evil. The unseen realm is more real than the physical world, and every prayer you pray engages in spiritual warfare.

This chapter will explore:

✅ How prayer fights spiritual battles

✅ What happens in the unseen realm when we pray

✅ How to use prayer as a weapon against the enemy

1. The Reality of Spiritual Warfare

📖 2 Corinthians 10:3-4 – "For though we walk in the flesh, we do not war according to the flesh. For the weapons of our warfare are not carnal but mighty in God for pulling down strongholds."

Many Christians do not realize that prayer is a battle strategy. When we pray, we are:

♦ Engaging in a war against the enemy.

♦ Strengthening God's kingdom on earth.

◆ Releasing God's power into situations.

The devil's greatest deception is convincing believers that prayer is weak. But in reality, prayer shifts atmospheres, releases angelic forces, and destroys demonic strongholds.

📖 Biblical Example: Jesus Resisting Satan in the Wilderness (Luke 4:1-13)

✅ Jesus fought the enemy using Scripture and prayer.

📖 Application: If Jesus used prayer to fight Satan, how much more do we need to?

2. How Does Prayer Fight Spiritual Battles?

◆ Prayer Releases God's Power

📖 Jeremiah 33:3 – "Call to Me, and I will answer you, and show you great and mighty things, which you do not know."

◆ When you pray, you activate God's intervention.

◆ Prayer releases God's authority into situations.

◆ Through prayer, heaven responds, and hell trembles.

📖 Biblical Example: Paul and Silas in Prison (Acts 16:25-26)

✅ They prayed, and God shook the prison with an earthquake!

◆ Prayer Stops the Enemy's Plans

📖 Isaiah 54:17 – "No weapon formed against you shall prosper."

◆ The enemy plots against God's people, but prayer blocks his attacks.

◆ Through prayer, satanic assignments are canceled.

◆ A praying believer is untouchable in the spirit realm.

📖 Biblical Example: Hezekiah's Prayer Against the Assyrians (2 Kings 19:14-36)

✓ Hezekiah prayed, and an angel destroyed 185,000 enemy soldiers!

◆ Prayer Releases Angelic Assistance

📖 Psalm 91:11 – "For He will command His angels concerning you to guard you in all your ways."

◆ Angels are dispatched when believers pray.

◆ They war against demonic forces to bring God's answers.

◆ Without prayer, angelic assistance is hindered.

📖 Biblical Example: Peter's Angelic Rescue (Acts 12:5-11)

✓ The church prayed, and an angel freed Peter from prison.

📖 Application: When you pray, heavenly armies move on your behalf.

3. What Happens in the Unseen Realm When We Pray?

📖 Daniel 10:12-14 – "From the first day that you set your heart to understand… your words were heard; and I have come because of your words. But the prince of Persia withstood me twenty-one days."

✓ Daniel's prayers caused warfare in the spirit realm.

✅ Angels battled demonic forces for 21 days to bring the answer.

✅ His prayer was the deciding factor in the spiritual battle.

◆ Prayer Weakens Demonic Forces

📖 Luke 10:19 – "I have given you authority to trample on snakes and scorpions and to overcome all the power of the enemy."

◆ When believers pray, demonic strongholds break.

◆ Prayer weakens the enemy's influence over lives and regions.

◆ The devil cannot stand against a prayerful Christian.

📖 Biblical Example: Jesus Casting Out Demons (Mark 9:29)

✅ Jesus said, "This kind can only come out by prayer and fasting."

📖 Application: Fasting adds firepower to your prayers in battle.

◆ Prayer Builds a Wall of Protection

📖 *Ezekiel 22:30* – "I looked for someone among them who would build up the wall and stand before me in the gap…"

◆ Prayer is standing in the gap for others.

◆ It prevents destruction and stops demonic invasions.

◆ Prayer surrounds families, cities, and nations with divine protection.

📖 Biblical Example: Abraham Interceding for Sodom (Genesis 18:22-33)

✅ Abraham prayed on behalf of the city, and God delayed judgment.

📖 Application: Who are you standing in the gap for through prayer?

4. How to Pray in Spiritual Warfare

◆ **Use the Name of Jesus**

📖 Philippians 2:10 – "At the name of Jesus every knee should bow, in heaven and on earth and under the earth."

✅ The name of Jesus carries ultimate authority.

✅ Demons tremble at His name.

✅ Pray in Jesus' name for maximum power.

◆ **Use the Word of God as a Sword**

📖 Hebrews 4:12 – "The Word of God is alive and active, sharper than any double-edged sword."

✅ The Bible is a weapon against the enemy.

✅ Speak scriptures aloud during prayer battles.

✅ Use verses that declare victory, healing, and deliverance.

📖 Biblical Example: Jesus Defeating Satan with Scripture (Matthew 4:1-11)

✅ Jesus said, "It is written…" and the devil had to flee.

📖 Application: Memorize verses that defeat the enemy's lies.

◆ **Pray in the Holy Spirit**

📖 Romans 8:26 – "The Spirit Himself intercedes for us with groanings too deep for words."

✅ The Holy Spirit helps us pray when we don't know what to say.

✅ Praying in tongues is a direct connection to the supernatural.

✅ The Spirit prays perfect prayers according to God's will.

📖 Biblical Example: The Early Church Praying in the Spirit (Acts 2:1-4)

✅ They were filled with power after praying in the Spirit.

📖 Application: If you pray in tongues, use it daily for breakthrough.

5. Signs of Victory in Spiritual Warfare

📖 James 5:16 – "The effective, fervent prayer of a righteous man avails much."

✅ Peace comes over your situation (Philippians 4:7).

✅ Demonic attacks lose their grip (Luke 10:19).

✅ Supernatural breakthroughs appear (Daniel 10:12).

📖 Biblical Example: Jehoshaphat's Victory Through Prayer (2 Chronicles 20:1-30)

✅ Jehoshaphat prayed, and God sent confusion into the enemy's camp.

📖 Application: If you're fighting a battle, keep praying until victory manifests.

6. Conclusion: Prayer Wins Every Battle

📖 2 Chronicles 7:14 – "If My people, who are called by My name, will humble themselves and pray and seek My face… I will hear from heaven."

🔥 **Prayer is more than communication—it is warfare.**

🔥 **When you pray, you shake the kingdom of darkness.**

🔥 **God has given you authority—use it!**

🏰 **Are you ready to fight battles through prayer and see victory?**

Chapter 7:
The Power of Persistent Prayer

📖 Luke 18:1 – "Men ought always to pray, and not to faint."

Prayer is not just about asking once and receiving instantly—it is about perseverance, faith, and endurance. Many believers pray for a short time, and when they don't see immediate results, they give up. However, the Bible teaches that persistence in prayer moves heaven, strengthens faith, and produces miraculous breakthroughs.

In this chapter, we will explore:

✅ Why God sometimes delays answers to prayer

✅ How persistence in prayer builds unwavering faith

✅ How to pray with endurance and expectation

1. Why Does God Sometimes Delay Answers?

📖 Habakkuk 2:3 – "For the vision is yet for an appointed time; though it tarry, wait for it; because it will surely come."

Many people misunderstand delayed answers in prayer. God's delays are not denials. Sometimes, the timing is not right. Other times, God is preparing something better than we asked for.

◆ Delays Build Spiritual Endurance

📖 James 1:3-4 – "The testing of your faith produces perseverance. Let perseverance finish its work so that you may be mature and complete, not lacking anything."

✅ God delays some prayers because He wants to strengthen our faith.

✅ Without waiting, we would never learn endurance.

✅ Faith grows strongest when it must persist through challenges.

📖 Biblical Example: Abraham and Sarah Waiting for Isaac (Genesis 21:1-7)

✅ God promised them a child, but they had to wait 25 years for the promise to be fulfilled.

📖 Application: If you are waiting for an answer, God is strengthening you for something greater.

◆ Delays Test the Sincerity of Our Prayers

📖 Jeremiah 29:13 – "You will seek Me and find Me when you seek Me with all your heart."

✅ Some people only pray when they desperately need something.

✅ God uses delays to test if we are truly seeking Him or just seeking His blessings.

✅ Persistent prayer reveals a heart that is fully devoted to God.

📖 Biblical Example: Hannah Praying for a Child (1 Samuel 1:10-20)

✅ Hannah cried out to God for years, and He finally gave her Samuel, one of Israel's greatest prophets.

📖 Application: Don't just pray for what you want—pray because you desire God's will above all else.

◆ Delays Align Our Desires with God's Will

📖 1 John 5:14-15 – "If we ask anything according to His will, He hears us."

✅ God is not obligated to answer every request instantly.

✅ He answers when our prayers align with His perfect will.

✅ The waiting process refines our desires and makes them God-centered.

📖 Biblical Example: Paul's "Thorn in the Flesh" (2 Corinthians 12:7-9)

✅ Paul prayed three times for healing, but God said, "My grace is sufficient for you."

📖 Application: Sometimes, instead of removing challenges, God gives us the grace to endure them.

2. The Power of Persistent Prayer

📖 *Matthew 7:7-8* – "Ask, and it will be given to you; seek, and you will find; knock, and it will be opened to you."

The words "ask, seek, knock" in Greek imply continuous action:

✅ Ask and keep asking.

✅ Seek and keep seeking.

✅ Knock and keep knocking.

Persistent prayer does not mean repeating empty words—it means praying with faith, determination, and expectation.

📖 Biblical Example: The Persistent Widow (Luke 18:1-8)

✅ She kept knocking until the unjust judge granted her request—how much more will God answer His children?

📖 Application: Faith-filled persistence brings results. Don't stop praying because you haven't seen an answer yet.

◆ **Persistence Produces Unshakable Faith**

📖 Romans 4:20-21 – "Abraham did not waver through unbelief regarding the promise of God, but was strengthened in faith, giving glory to God."

✅ Faith grows stronger when it must endure opposition.

✅ Persistent prayer teaches trust and dependence on God.

✅ Breakthroughs often come at the moment when we are about to give up.

📖 Biblical Example: Elijah Praying for Rain (1 Kings 18:41-45)

✅ Elijah prayed seven times before the rain came—he refused to stop until he saw results.

📖 Application: Never stop praying for your breakthrough. Keep pressing until heaven moves.

◆ The Enemy Tries to Discourage Persistent Prayer

📖 Daniel 10:12-13 – "From the first day that you set your heart to understand and humble yourself before your God, your words were heard, and I have come in response to them. But the prince of Persia resisted me twenty-one days."

✓ Daniel's prayer was heard immediately, but spiritual warfare delayed the answer.

✓ Some answers take time because the enemy fights against them.

✓ Persistent prayer breaks demonic resistance and allows God's will to manifest.

📖 Application: Spiritual warfare is real—don't let delays make you doubt God.

3. Real-Life Testimonies of Persistent Prayer

◆ A Businessman Who Prayed for 10 Years Before Breakthrough

✓ A Christian businessman felt God's calling to start a company, but for 10 years he faced failure after failure.

✓ Instead of giving up, he prayed daily, fasting and seeking God's direction.

✓ After 10 years of persistence, a divine connection led to a contract that transformed his company overnight.

✅ God used the waiting period to develop his patience, wisdom, and faith.

📖 Application: God will answer in the right season. Keep believing!

◆ A Mother Who Prayed 20 Years for Her Son's Salvation

✅ A mother never stopped praying for her rebellious son.

✅ For 20 years, he rejected God and lived in sin.

✅ One day, in a crisis, he remembered her prayers and turned back to Christ.

✅ Now, he is a pastor, leading thousands to Jesus.

📖 Application: No prayer is wasted. Keep interceding for your loved ones!

4. How to Develop Persistent Prayer in Your Life

📖 *Colossians 4:2* – "Devote yourselves to prayer, being watchful and thankful."

🔥 How can you stay persistent in prayer?

◆ 1. Set a Daily Prayer Habit

✅ Schedule specific times each day for prayer.

✅ Consistency is key—even when you don't feel like praying.

✅ Build spiritual discipline like Daniel, who prayed three times a day (Daniel 6:10).

◆ 2. Pray with Scripture

📖 Isaiah 55:11 – "My word will not return to Me void."

✅ Use Bible verses to strengthen your prayers.

✅ God honors His Word—pray His promises back to Him.

📖 Example: If praying for healing, declare Isaiah 53:5: "By His stripes, I am healed."

◆ 3. Join a Prayer Community

📖 Matthew 18:19-20 – "If two of you agree on earth about anything they ask, it will be done."

✅ Find prayer partners to keep you encouraged.

✅ Corporate prayer increases spiritual power.

✅ Churches that pray together see more miracles.

◆ 4. Fast and Pray for Breakthroughs

📖 Matthew 17:21 – "This kind does not go out except by prayer and fasting."

✅ Fasting adds power to your prayers.

✅ It helps you focus on God and not distractions.

📖 Biblical Example: Esther Fasting for Victory (Esther 4:16)

✅ Her three-day fast changed the course of history.

5. Conclusion: Never Stop Praying!

📖 1 Thessalonians 5:17 – "Pray without ceasing."

🔥 **Prayer works, but persistence is key!**

🔥 **Don't stop just because the answer hasn't come yet!**

🔥 **Keep believing—your breakthrough is coming!**

🛍 **Are you ready to develop a powerful, persistent prayer life?**

Chapter 8:
The Power of Agreement in Prayer

📖 Matthew 18:19-20 – "Again, I say unto you, that if two of you shall agree on earth as touching anything that they shall ask, it shall be done for them by My Father which is in heaven. For where two or three are gathered together in My name, there am I in the midst of them."

One of the most overlooked yet powerful principles of prayer is the power of agreement. Many believers pray alone, which is important, but the Bible reveals that corporate prayer—prayer in agreement with others—carries extraordinary power.

In this chapter, we will explore:

✅ Why corporate prayer is so powerful

✅ How unity in prayer unlocks supernatural breakthroughs

✅ Why having prayer partners can change your spiritual life

1. Why is Corporate Prayer So Powerful?

📖 *Ecclesiastes 4:9-12* – "Two are better than one, because they have a good return for their labor... Though one may be overpowered, two can defend themselves. A cord of three strands is not quickly broken."

Praying alone is **essential**, but when believers unite in prayer, the **spiritual atmosphere shifts**.

◆ Corporate Prayer Invites the Presence of God

📖 Psalm 133:1-3 – "Behold, how good and how pleasant it is for brethren to dwell together in unity… For there the Lord commanded the blessing."

✅ God commands a blessing when His people pray in unity.

✅ His presence becomes tangible when believers agree in faith.

📖 Biblical Example: Pentecost and the Outpouring of the Holy Spirit (Acts 2:1-4)

✅ The disciples were praying in unity, and the Holy Spirit filled them with power.

📖 Application: When churches, families, and friends pray together, they invite heaven's presence and power.

◆ Agreement in Prayer Strengthens Faith

📖 Hebrews 10:24-25 – "Let us consider how we may spur one another on toward love and good deeds, not giving up meeting together."

✅ When believers pray together, their faith strengthens.

✅ Doubt is weakened when surrounded by faith-filled people.

✅ Corporate prayer builds courage to believe for impossible things.

📖 Biblical Example: Moses, Aaron, and Hur Holding Up the Staff (Exodus 17:8-13)

✓ Moses prayed alone, but his strength wavered.

✓ Aaron and Hur lifted his arms, and Israel won the battle.

📖 Application: Do you have people who hold you up in prayer?

2. How Does Agreement Unlock God's Power?

📖 Acts 1:14 – "They all joined together constantly in prayer, along with the women and Mary the mother of Jesus, and with His brothers."

When believers pray in agreement, it opens the door for God's supernatural **intervention**.

◆ Unified Prayer Shakes the Spiritual Realm

📖 Acts 4:23-31 – "After they prayed, the place where they were meeting was shaken. And they were all filled with the Holy Spirit and spoke the word of God boldly."

✓ The early church faced persecution, but when they prayed in unity, heaven responded.

✓ The ground literally shook, and they were filled with boldness.

✓ Corporate prayer activates miracles and bold faith.

📖 Biblical Example: Jehoshaphat's Prayer Army (2 Chronicles 20:1-22)

✓ The people gathered to pray, and God sent confusion into the enemy's camp.

📖 Application: Agreement in prayer is not just about numbers—it's about faith-filled unity.

◆ Prayer in Agreement Produces Breakthroughs

📖 James 5:16 – "The prayer of a righteous person is powerful and effective."

✅ When righteous believers agree in prayer, things shift.

✅ God honors faith-filled agreement.

✅ Persistent, unified prayer opens doors that were previously shut.

📖 Biblical Example: Peter's Angelic Rescue (Acts 12:5-17)

✅ Peter was in prison, but the church prayed for him without ceasing.

✅ An angel broke his chains and led him out.

✅ Their corporate prayers unlocked divine intervention.

📖 Application: If you are facing a battle, gather believers to stand with you in prayer.

3. The Power of Prayer Partnerships

📖 Deuteronomy 32:30 – "One can chase a thousand, and two can put ten thousand to flight."

Prayer multiplies in power when believers partner in faith.

◆ Finding a Prayer Partner Can Transform Your Life

✅ A prayer partner holds you accountable.

✅ Praying together keeps your faith strong in trials.

✅ Iron sharpens iron—praying together strengthens both believers.

📖 Biblical Example: Paul and Silas in Prison (Acts 16:25-26)

✅ They prayed and worshiped together.

✅ An earthquake came, and their chains were broken.

📖 Application: Do you have someone who prays with you regularly?

◆ **Why Every Church Needs a Strong Prayer Ministry**

📖 1 Timothy 2:1-2 – "I urge, then, first of all, that petitions, prayers, intercession and thanksgiving be made for all people."

✅ Churches that pray together see more miracles.

✅ Revival always starts with united prayer.

✅ A praying church is a strong church.

📖 Biblical Example: The Moravian Prayer Revival (1727)

✅ A small community began **24/7 prayer**, and revival spread worldwide.

📖 Application: Every believer should be part of a prayer group.

4. How to Pray in Agreement with Power

📖 *Colossians 4:2* – "Devote yourselves to prayer, being watchful and thankful."

🔥 **How can you pray in agreement effectively?**

◆ **1. Pray Aloud Together**

📖 Acts 4:24 – "They raised their voices together in prayer to God."

✔ Speak boldly in unity.

✔ Prayer is powerful when spoken with conviction.

◆ **2. Stand on God's Word**

📖 Isaiah 55:11 – "My word… shall not return to Me void."

✔ Declare God's promises aloud.

✔ The Bible strengthens prayer in agreement.

📖 Example: If praying for healing, declare Isaiah 53:5: "By His stripes, we are healed."

◆ **3. Set Prayer Goals Together**

📖 Habakkuk 2:2 – "Write the vision; make it plain on tablets."

✔ Write down prayer requests.

✔ Track answered prayers to build faith.

◆ **4. Don't Stop Until the Answer Comes**

📖 Luke 11:9-10 – "Keep asking, and it will be given to you; keep seeking, and you will find; keep knocking, and the door will be opened."

✅ Agreement prayer requires persistence.

✅ Don't stop until you see the breakthrough.

📖 Biblical Example: Elijah Praying for Rain (1 Kings 18:41-45)

✅ He prayed seven times before the rain came.

5. Conclusion: Agreement Prayer Changes Everything!

📖 Matthew 18:19-20 – "If two of you shall agree… it shall be done."

🔥 **Prayer in agreement multiplies results!**

🔥 **Corporate prayer shifts atmospheres!**

🔥 **Find people to pray with and see breakthroughs!**

👥 **Who can you partner with in prayer today?**

Chapter 9:
Praying with Authority and Boldness

📖 Hebrews 4:16 – "Let us therefore come boldly unto the throne of grace, that we may obtain mercy, and find grace to help in time of need."

One of the greatest privileges believers have is the ability to approach God with boldness. However, many Christians struggle with confidence in prayer. They may pray timidly, unsure if God will answer, or they may not understand the authority they have in Christ.

In this chapter, we will explore:

✅ How to develop confidence in prayer

✅ Why some prayers lack authority

✅ How bold, faith-filled prayers shift spiritual atmospheres

1. How Do We Develop Confidence in Prayer?

📖 1 John 5:14-15 – "This is the confidence we have in approaching God: that if we ask anything according to His will, He hears us. And if we know that He hears us—whatever we ask—we know that we have what we asked of Him."

Confidence in prayer comes from knowing who we are in Christ and believing that God hears us.

◆ Confidence is Rooted in Our Identity in Christ

📖 Romans 8:15 – "For you have not received a spirit of bondage again to fear, but you have received the Spirit of adoption, whereby we cry, 'Abba, Father.'"

✅ We are children of God, not strangers or outsiders.

✅ A child has direct access to their father—so do we with God.

📖 Biblical Example: The Prodigal Son's Restoration (Luke 15:11-32)

✅ Though the son had failed, his father embraced him with love.

✅ Likewise, God welcomes us with open arms when we pray.

📖 Application: Confidence in prayer grows when we realize we are already accepted by God.

◆ Confidence is Strengthened by Knowing God's Word

📖 Romans 10:17 – "Faith comes by hearing, and hearing by the Word of God."

✅ The more we know God's promises, the bolder our prayers become.

✅ Praying Scripture increases confidence and authority.

📖 Biblical Example: Joshua Declaring Victory (Joshua 1:8-9)

✅ God told Joshua to meditate on His Word to have success.

📖 Application: If you want to pray with boldness, start by reading and declaring God's Word.

◆ **Confidence Grows Through Experience**

📖 Psalm 34:4 – "I sought the Lord, and He answered me; He delivered me from all my fears."

✅ The more we pray and see God answer, the stronger our confidence becomes.

✅ Small victories lead to bigger faith.

📖 Biblical Example: David's Growing Confidence (1 Samuel 17:34-37)

✅ David's victories over the lion and bear gave him faith to defeat Goliath.

📖 Application: Start praying boldly in small matters, and you will develop faith for bigger ones.

2. Why Do Some Prayers Lack Authority?

📖 James 1:6-7 – "But let him ask in faith, nothing wavering. For he that wavers is like a wave of the sea, driven with the wind and tossed. That person should not expect to receive anything from the Lord."

Some prayers lack power because they are not prayed with faith and authority.

◆ **Authority Requires Knowing Our Position in Christ**

📖 *Luke 10:19* – "Behold, I give unto you power to tread on serpents and scorpions, and over all the power of the enemy: and nothing shall by any means hurt you."

✅ Many Christians pray weak prayers because they do not realize they have been given authority.

✅ Jesus defeated Satan and gave believers spiritual authority to pray with power.

📖 Biblical Example: Peter and John Healing the Lame Man (Acts 3:1-10)

✅ They did not beg God for healing—they commanded healing in Jesus' name.

📖 Application: Stop praying passively—start praying with kingdom authority.

◆ Authority Requires Alignment with God's Will

📖 John 15:7 – "If you abide in Me, and My words abide in you, ask whatever you wish, and it will be done for you."

✅ Authority comes from being aligned with God's will.

✅ Many prayers lack power because they are selfish or misaligned with God's purpose.

📖 Biblical Example: Jesus in Gethsemane (Luke 22:42)

✅ Jesus prayed, "Not My will, but Yours be done."

📖 Application: Pray according to God's will, and your prayers will have power.

3. Praying with Boldness Like Jesus

📖 Mark 11:24 – "Therefore I tell you, whatever you ask for in prayer, believe that you have received it, and it will be yours."

Jesus prayed bold, authoritative prayers—and He is our model.

◆ Jesus Spoke Bold Prayers with Authority

📖 *John 11:41-43* – "Father, I thank You that You have heard Me. I knew that You always hear Me… Lazarus, come forth!"

✅ Jesus prayed with confidence, not doubt.

✅ He did not beg—He declared God's will boldly.

📖 Application: Speak prayers that align with God's Word and expect results.

◆ Bold Prayers Release Miracles

📖 Acts 4:29-31 – "Now, Lord, consider their threats and enable Your servants to speak Your word with great boldness… After they prayed, the place where they were meeting was shaken."

✅ Bold prayers shake the spiritual realm.

✅ When believers pray with courage and authority, miracles happen.

📖 Biblical Example: Elijah Calling Down Fire (1 Kings 18:36-38)

✅ Elijah did not doubt—he declared God's power, and fire fell from heaven.

📖 Application: Stop praying timid prayers—start praying bold, faith-filled prayers.

4. What Happens in the Spirit When We Pray with Authority?

📖 Matthew 16:19 – "I will give you the keys of the kingdom of heaven; whatever you bind on earth will be bound in heaven, and whatever you loose on earth will be loosed in heaven."

When believers pray with authority and boldness, powerful things happen in the spiritual realm.

◆ Bold Prayers Bind and Loose in the Spiritual Realm

📖 Ephesians 6:12 – "For we wrestle not against flesh and blood, but against principalities, against powers, against the rulers of the darkness of this world."

✓ Prayer has the power to bind the works of the enemy.

✓ Spiritual warfare is won through bold declarations in prayer.

📖 Biblical Example: Paul Casting Out a Demon (Acts 16:16-18)

✓ Paul did not pray timidly—he commanded the spirit to leave in Jesus' name.

📖 Application: Speak bold prayers of deliverance and breakthrough.

◆ Prayer Unlocks Angelic Assistance

📖 Daniel 10:12-13 – "Your words were heard, and I have come in response to them. But the prince of Persia resisted me twenty-one days."

✅ Bold prayers release angelic intervention.

✅ Spiritual resistance can delay answers, but persistence wins the battle.

📖 Biblical Example: Peter's Angelic Escape (Acts 12:5-10)

✅ The church prayed without ceasing, and an angel released Peter from prison.

📖 Application: Bold, persistent prayer shifts spiritual realities.

5. Conclusion: Pray Boldly and Expect Miracles

📖 Hebrews 4:16 – "Come boldly unto the throne of grace."

🔥 **Pray with confidence—God hears you!**

🔥 **Declare His promises and expect results!**

🔥 **Your bold prayers shift spiritual atmospheres!**

📕 **Are you ready to pray with authority and boldness?**

Chapter 10:
The Joy of Answered Prayer

📖 Psalm 37:4 – "Delight yourself in the Lord, and He will give you the desires of your heart."

There is no greater joy than experiencing an answered prayer. When we cry out to God and see Him move in our lives, our faith deepens, our hearts are strengthened, and we realize that we serve a God who hears and responds.

Yet, many believers struggle with discouragement when prayers seem unanswered or delayed. In this chapter, we will explore:

✅ The joy that comes when God answers our prayers

✅ Why some prayers take time to be fulfilled

✅ How to maintain faith and joy while waiting

1. Answered Prayer Reveals God's Faithfulness

📖 Jeremiah 33:3 – "Call unto Me, and I will answer you, and show you great and mighty things, which you do not know."

God delights in answering the prayers of His children. His responses are not based on random chance but on His love, wisdom, and perfect timing.

◆ God's Character is One of Faithfulness

📖 Numbers 23:19 – "God is not a man, that He should lie; neither the son of man, that He should repent. Has He said, and shall He not do it? Or has He spoken, and shall He not make it good?"

✅ God never breaks His promises.

✅ Every answered prayer is a testament to His trustworthiness.

📖 Biblical Example: God Answering Abraham and Sarah's Prayer (Genesis 21:1-7)

✅ After years of waiting, God fulfilled His promise and gave them Isaac.

✅ God does not forget prayers—even those prayed long ago.

📖 Application: When God answers prayers, rejoice in His faithfulness and trust Him for even greater things.

2. Why Some Prayers Take Time to be Answered

📖 Habakkuk 2:3 – "For the vision is yet for an appointed time; but at the end it shall speak, and not lie: though it tarries, wait for it; because it will surely come."

Sometimes, we pray and do not receive immediate answers. This does not mean God is ignoring us—it means that there is a divine reason for the delay.

◆ God's Timing is Perfect

📖 Ecclesiastes 3:11 – "He has made everything beautiful in its time."

✅ God knows when the right time is for a prayer to be fulfilled.

✅ A delayed answer does not mean denied—it means wait and trust.

📖 Biblical Example: Joseph's Delayed Destiny (Genesis 37-50)

✅ Joseph had dreams of greatness, but his journey included betrayal, slavery, and prison.

✅ Yet, God's plan was at work the entire time, and at the right moment, Joseph became ruler of Egypt.

📖 Application: If your prayer is delayed, trust that God is preparing you for something greater.

◆ Sometimes, God's "No" is a Blessing

📖 2 Corinthians 12:9 – "My grace is sufficient for you, for My power is made perfect in weakness."

✅ Not every prayer is answered the way we expect.

✅ Sometimes, God says "No" or "Not Yet" because He has something better planned.

📖 Biblical Example: Paul's Thorn in the Flesh (2 Corinthians 12:7-10)

✅ Paul prayed three times for his affliction to be removed, but God allowed it to remain.

✅ Instead of removing it, God gave him grace and strength to endure.

📖 Application: Trust that God's ways are higher than ours and that even unanswered prayers can be part of His greater plan.

3. The Joy of Receiving a Long-Awaited Answer

📖 Psalm 30:5 – "Weeping may endure for a night, but joy comes in the morning."

There is great joy when prayers are answered after years of waiting.

📖 Biblical Example: Hannah's Joy When God Answered Her Prayer (1 Samuel 2:1-10)

✔ Hannah was barren and prayed desperately for a child.

✔ After years of waiting, God answered and gave her Samuel, who became a prophet of Israel.

✔ Hannah's prayer of thanksgiving is a beautiful example of rejoicing in answered prayers.

📖 1 Samuel 2:1 – "My heart rejoices in the Lord; in the Lord, my horn is lifted high."

📖 Testimony: A Couple's Miracle Baby After Years of Prayer

✔ A couple struggled with infertility for over a decade.

✔ Doctors gave up, but they continued to pray and trust God.

✔ After years of believing, they conceived naturally and had a healthy baby.

📖 Application: When prayers are answered, give thanks and share your testimony—it builds faith in others!

4. Rejoicing Even Before the Answer Comes

📖 Philippians 4:6-7 – "Do not be anxious about anything, but in every situation, by prayer and petition, with thanksgiving, present your requests to God."

Faith-filled believers learn to rejoice in prayer even before they see the answer.

◆ Thanksgiving Prepares the Way for Breakthrough

📖 1 Thessalonians 5:18 – "Give thanks in all circumstances; for this is God's will for you in Christ Jesus."

✓ Thanking God before the answer comes is an act of faith.

✓ Gratitude creates a posture of expectation and trust.

📖 Biblical Example: Jehoshaphat's Worship Before the Battle (2 Chronicles 20:21-22)

✓ Instead of sending soldiers first, Jehoshaphat sent worshippers into battle.

✓ As they praised God, the enemy was defeated before they even fought.

📖 Application: Don't wait until your prayer is answered to rejoice—start worshipping in advance!

5. Celebrating the Joy of Answered Prayer with Others

📖 Romans 12:15 – "Rejoice with those who rejoice."

The joy of answered prayer is meant to be shared. When God answers your prayers, it encourages others to believe for their own miracles.

◆ Testimonies Build Faith

📖 Revelation 12:11 – "They overcame him by the blood of the Lamb, and by the word of their testimony."

✓ Sharing answered prayers inspires faith in others.

✓ Every testimony is proof that God is still working today.

📖 Biblical Example: The Leper Who Came Back to Thank Jesus (Luke 17:15-19)

✓ Ten lepers were healed, but only one returned to give thanks.

✓ Jesus said, "Your faith has made you whole."

📖 Application: When God answers your prayers, don't keep it to yourself—share it with others to bring glory to God!

6. Conclusion: God Still Answers Prayers Today!

📖 *Matthew 7:7* – "Ask, and it will be given to you; seek, and you will find; knock, and the door will be opened to you."

🔥 **Answered prayers bring joy, strengthen faith, and glorify God.**

🔥 **Trust in His timing, rejoice in His faithfulness, and never stop believing!**

🔥 **Share your testimony so others can believe for their own miracles!**

📕 **What answered prayer are you celebrating today?**

Chapter 11:
Prayer as a Lifestyle

📖 Colossians 4:2 – "Continue steadfastly in prayer, being watchful in it with thanksgiving."

Prayer is not meant to be an occasional act but a continuous, life-giving connection with God. Many believers only pray in moments of crisis, but Scripture teaches that prayer should be as natural as breathing. It is not just a spiritual discipline—it is a way of life.

This chapter will explore:

✅ How Jesus modeled a lifestyle of prayer

✅ Why prayer must be consistent, not just situational

✅ How to build a strong, daily prayer habit

1. Jesus' Consistent Prayer Life

📖 Mark 1:35 – "And in the morning, rising up a great while before day, He went out, and departed into a solitary place, and there prayed."

Jesus, the Son of God, never neglected prayer. If He—being sinless and full of wisdom—needed to pray constantly, how much more should we?

◆ Jesus Prayed Before Major Decisions

📖 Luke 6:12-13 – "One day soon afterward Jesus went up on a mountain to pray, and He prayed to God all night. At daybreak, He

71

called together all of His disciples and chose twelve of them to be apostles."

✓ Before choosing the twelve disciples, Jesus spent an entire night in prayer.

✓ Major decisions require seeking God's guidance through prayer.

📖 Biblical Example: Jesus Praying in Gethsemane (Matthew 26:36-44)

✓ In His most difficult moment, Jesus prayed fervently for strength to fulfill His mission.

✓ His consistent prayer life prepared Him for the greatest challenge—going to the cross.

📖 Application: Before making big life decisions, spend time in focused prayer like Jesus did.

2. Prayer Must Be Consistent, Not Just Situational

📖 1 Thessalonians 5:17 – "Pray without ceasing."

Many believers only pray when they need something. But true spiritual maturity is developed when prayer becomes a natural part of everyday life.

◆ The Early Church Prayed Constantly

📖 Acts 2:42 – "They devoted themselves to the apostles' teaching and to fellowship, to the breaking of bread and to prayer."

✅ The early church was built on prayer—it was not just something they did occasionally.

✅ Their consistent prayer life led to miracles, unity, and revival.

📖 Biblical Example: Daniel's Daily Prayer Habit (Daniel 6:10)

✅ Even when praying was illegal, Daniel prayed three times a day.

✅ His faithfulness in prayer led to divine protection in the lion's den.

📖 Application: Make prayer a priority, not just an emergency response.

3. How to Build a Strong, Daily Prayer Habit

📖 Matthew 6:6 – "But when you pray, go into your room, close the door and pray to your Father, who is unseen."

A strong prayer life is built through intentional discipline and consistency.

◆ Set a Specific Time for Prayer

✅ Jesus often prayed in the morning (Mark 1:35).

✅ Daniel prayed three times a day (Daniel 6:10).

✅ Find a time that works best for you and commit to it daily.

📖 Application: Schedule prayer just as you would schedule important meetings—because meeting with God is the most important thing.

◆ **Pray with a Purpose**

✓ Follow the **Lord's Prayer model** (*Matthew 6:9-13*):

1. **Worship God** ("Our Father in heaven, hallowed be Your name")
2. **Pray for His will** ("Your kingdom come, Your will be done")
3. **Ask for provision** ("Give us this day our daily bread")
4. **Seek forgiveness and forgive others** ("Forgive us our debts")
5. **Pray for protection** ("Deliver us from the evil one")

📖 Application: Use this model as a foundation to strengthen your prayer life.

◆ **Keep a Prayer Journal**

✓ Writing down prayers, scriptures, and testimonies helps build faith.

✓ Seeing past answered prayers reminds you of God's faithfulness.

📖 Biblical Example: The Psalms as Prayers (Book of Psalms)

✓ King David wrote his prayers and praises, which became a testimony for generations.

📖 Application: Write down your prayers and track God's responses.

◆ **Engage in a 21-Day Prayer Challenge**

📖 Psalm 119:105 – "Your word is a lamp to my feet and a light to my path."

To help establish prayer as a daily habit, commit to a 21-day prayer challenge.

✅ Week 1 – Building the Habit

- Pray for 10 minutes each morning and night.
- Use a prayer journal to write your prayers.
- Meditate on one prayer-related scripture per day.

✅ Week 2 – Deepening the Connection

- Increase prayer time to 20 minutes.
- Pray with specific requests and thank God for what He has already done.
- Find a prayer partner and pray together.

✅ Week 3 – Transforming Prayer into a Lifestyle

- Pray for 30 minutes daily.
- Incorporate prayer walks and worship into your routine.
- Fast from distractions (social media, TV) and replace them with prayer time.

📖 Application: By the end of 21 days, prayer will feel natural and life-giving!

4. The Transformational Power of a Lifestyle of Prayer

📖 James 5:16 – "The prayer of a righteous person is powerful and effective."

A lifestyle of prayer will:

✅ Draw you closer to God

✅ Strengthen your faith

✅ Give you peace and clarity

✅ Release God's power over your life

📖 Biblical Example: Cornelius' Consistent Prayers (Acts 10:1-4)

✅ Cornelius prayed regularly, and an angel appeared to him with a divine message.

✅ Consistent prayer opens doors for supernatural encounters.

📖 Application: Make prayer your first response, not your last resort.

5. Conclusion: Will You Commit to a Life of Prayer?

📖 Luke 11:9 – "Ask, and it will be given to you; seek, and you will find; knock, and it will be opened to you."

🔥 **Prayer should not be occasional—it should be a lifestyle!**

🔥 **Jesus modeled continuous prayer—we must do the same!**

🔥 **If you commit to daily prayer, your life will never be the same!**

🏰 **Will you take the 21-Day Prayer Challenge?**

Chapter 12:
The Eternal Impact of Prayer

📖 Revelation 5:8 – "The prayers of the saints are incense before God."

Prayer is not just an act that affects the present moment—it has eternal consequences. Every prayer spoken in faith, alignment with God's will, and perseverance leaves a lasting impact in both the natural and spiritual realms. Many believers do not realize that their prayers outlive them, setting future generations up for blessings, breakthroughs, and divine intervention.

This chapter will explore:

✅ How prayer reaches into eternity

✅ The legacy of prayer in the Bible

✅ How our prayers impact heaven and future generations

1. Prayer Reaches Beyond Time

📖 Revelation 8:3-4 – "Another angel came and stood at the altar, holding a golden censer; and much incense was given to him, so that he might add it to the prayers of all the saints on the golden altar which was before the throne."

God does not forget prayers. The Bible reveals that prayers are stored in heaven and become a fragrant offering before God. This means that even when we do not immediately see the answers to our prayers, they continue working in the spiritual realm.

◆ Our Prayers Are Eternal

📖 Psalm 141:2 – "Let my prayer be set forth before you as incense, and the lifting up of my hands as the evening sacrifice."

✅ Prayers are not lost or forgotten.

✅ Even after a believer's life on earth has ended, their prayers continue producing results.

📖 Biblical Example: Simeon and Anna's Prayers for the Messiah (Luke 2:25-38)

✅ These two righteous individuals spent years in prayer, believing for the coming of the Messiah.

✅ Their prayers were fulfilled when they saw baby Jesus at the temple.

✅ Their prayers outlived their years of waiting.

📖 Application: When you pray, understand that your prayers are stored in heaven and will continue working even after you are gone.

2. The Legacy of Prayer in the Bible

📖 Acts 10:1-4 – "Cornelius, a centurion, a devout man who feared God… prayed continually to God. About the ninth hour of the day, he saw an angel of God."

Cornelius' prayers and devotion did not just affect his life—they brought salvation to his household. His consistency in prayer opened a divine door that led to an entire family encountering Jesus Christ.

◆ Prayers Can Change Generations

✅ Cornelius' prayers caused Peter to receive a vision and be sent to his home.

✅ Because of one man's prayers, the Gospel was opened to the Gentiles for the first time.

📖 Biblical Example: Hannah's Prayer for a Son (1 Samuel 1:10-20)

✅ Hannah prayed persistently for a child.

✅ Her son, Samuel, became a prophet who anointed King David.

✅ Her prayer impacted the future of Israel!

📖 Application: Your prayers have the power to shape your family, your community, and even nations.

3. How Prayer Impacts Heaven

📖 Matthew 6:10 – "Your kingdom come, your will be done, on earth as it is in heaven."

Prayer is not just communication—it is a spiritual weapon that releases heaven's will onto the earth. Every time we pray, we invite heaven's intervention into our lives and the world around us.

◆ Prayer Invokes Angelic Assistance

📖 Daniel 10:12-13 – "From the first day that you set your heart to understand… your words were heard, and I have come because of your words."

✅ When Daniel prayed, God sent angels to act on his behalf.

✓ Prayer engages heaven's armies to fight on our behalf.

📖 Biblical Example: Peter's Prison Breakthrough (Acts 12:5-10)

✓ The church prayed earnestly for Peter when he was imprisoned.

✓ An angel was sent to break his chains and lead him out of prison.

✓ Without prayer, he would have remained captive.

📖 Application: Prayer is not passive—it moves heaven and brings divine intervention!

4. Why We Must Keep Praying, Even When We Don't See Results

📖 *Galatians 6:9* – "Let us not grow weary in doing good, for in due season we will reap, if we do not give up."

Many believers **stop praying** when they don't see **immediate results**. However, Scripture reminds us that **prayers are seeds planted in faith**—they **will bear fruit in God's timing**.

◆ Delayed Answers Are Not Denied Answers

📖 Habakkuk 2:3 – "For the vision is yet for an appointed time… though it tarries, wait for it; because it will surely come."

✓ God's timing is perfect—our job is to pray in faith and trust His process.

📖 Biblical Example: Abraham and Sarah Waiting for Isaac (Genesis 21:1-7)

✅ They waited 25 years for the promise of a son to be fulfilled.

✅ God kept His word, even when it seemed impossible.

📖 Application: Even if you don't see results right away, keep praying—God is always working behind the scenes.

5. The Power of Intercessory Prayer

📖 1 Timothy 2:1 – "I urge, then, first of all, that petitions, prayers, intercession and thanksgiving be made for all people."

Intercessory prayer is standing in the gap for others. When we pray for people, families, cities, and nations, we invite God's intervention into their lives.

◆ Intercessory Prayer Can Shift Nations

📖 2 Chronicles 7:14 – "If My people, who are called by My name, will humble themselves and pray and seek My face… then I will hear from heaven and will forgive their sin and heal their land."

✅ Nations have been spared because of prayer.

✅ Revival has come through the prayers of God's people.

📖 Biblical Example: Moses Praying for Israel (Exodus 32:11-14)

✅ When Israel sinned, Moses interceded on their behalf.

✅ God relented from destroying them because of Moses' prayers.

📖 Application: Your prayers for others can bring healing, restoration, and breakthrough.

81

6. Conclusion: Your Prayers Are Eternal

📖 Luke 11:9 – "Ask, and it will be given to you; seek, and you will find; knock, and the door will be opened to you."

🔥 **Prayer is not just about the present—it builds an eternal legacy.**

🔥 **Your prayers are stored in heaven and continue working even after you are gone.**

🔥 **The more you pray, the more you invite heaven's power into the world.**

🏰 **Will you commit to leaving a legacy of prayer?**

www.ingramcontent.com/pod-product-compliance
Lightning Source LLC
LaVergne TN
LVHW052036080426
835513LV00018B/2350